PUB
SIGNS

ARTHUR CHAPPELL

AMBERLEY

This book is dedicated to Chris Brooks, Chris Cowan, The Inn Sign Society,
Kimberley Edmunds, David J. Howe, Nancy Kearney, Gill Marsland, Smuzz and Eira Short,
and Rebecca Wenham.

In Memoriam
Mike Don, David Johnson, Derek McDonald and Charles Partington

First published 2024

Amberley Publishing
The Hill, Stroud
Gloucestershire, GL5 4EP

www.amberley-books.com

Copyright © Arthur Chappell, 2024

The right of Arthur Chappell to be identified
as the Author of this work has been asserted in
accordance with the Copyrights, Designs and
Patents Act 1988.

ISBN 978 1 3981 1572 9 (print)
ISBN 978 1 3981 1573 6 (ebook)

British Library Cataloguing in Publication Data.
A catalogue record for this book is available from
the British Library.

Origination by Amberley Publishing.
Printed in the UK.

Introduction

Many inn signs are true works of art, worthy of display beside the best in the Tate or National Gallery. Studying them, however, can be challenging. A sign for The Bull (or Black Bull, White Bull and other variations) often literally shows a farm bull, even if the pub drew its name from papal Vatican bulletins ('bulls') sent to churches across Europe ensuring that the humblest village chapel followed the official doctrines of Rome. Sign creators, oblivious to this, or unsure how to represent it, simply painted agricultural bulls.

Signs can also relate to local or historic events, personalities, etc. Others use puns, riddles and humour. Some signs break the rules, others bear mistakes and some overlook the pub's more interesting stories.

When looking at the signs featured in this book, ask what you think is going on and then read the text to see if you were on the right track. It's not always as obvious as you might assume, there being a diverse range of themes explored, including history, mythology, crime, comedy, cheese and even dinosaurs.

The Adswood Hotel, No. 60 Adswood Lane, West Cale Green, Stockport, SK3 8HZ
Derived from Adder's Wood and giving Garden of Eden vibes, which is unsurprising given that the pub was originally called The Adam And Eve. (Author's image)

The Advocate, No. 7 Hunter Square, Edinburgh, EH1 1QW
The Advocate featuring *Rumpole of the Bailey*'s Horace Rumpole as portrayed by Leo McKern. Note the 'Called to the Bar' pun.

Aeronaut, No. 264 High Street, Acton, London, W3 9BH
Tightrope walking under a hot-air balloon – dangerous! The pub is named after a very different aerial daredevil: George Lee Temple, the first pilot to ever fly a plane upside down. (Author's image)

The Albert and the Lion, Bank Hey Street, Blackpool, FY1 4RU
Marriott Edgar's 1932 comedic monologue 'The Lion and Albert' tells of a child called Albert who tormented the zoo's aged, toothless lion, Wallace, even forcing its jaws open with a stick, until Wallace loses patience and swallows Albert whole. The poem focuses on Albert's parents complaining to the zookeepers. (Author's image)

THE ALICE LISLE

The Alice Lisle, Rockford Green, Rockford, Ringwood, BH24 3NA
Following arrest for hiding fugitives after the doomed Monmouth Rebellion of 1685, Lady Alice Lisle became the last woman executed by decapitation in England.

THE ANCIENT MARINER

The Ancient Mariner, Church Street, Workington, Cumbria, CA14 2HF
Not the albatross-slaying protagonist of Coleridge's poem (who never had an artificial leg) but a more generic sailor figure.

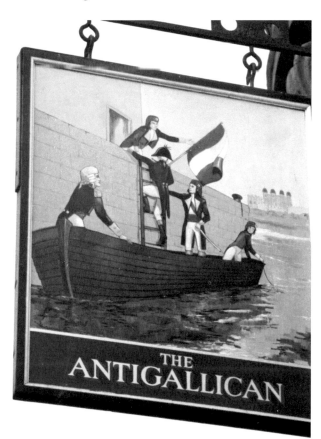

The Antigallican, No. 428
Woolwich Road, Charlton,
SE7 8SU
The Antigallican (Anti-French)
Society founded in 1775
was understandably popular
throughout the Napoleonic
Wars. This was one of the last
bars to retain the name.

The Astolat, No. 9 Old Palace
Road, Guildford, GU2 7TU
Astolat Castle was the legendary
prison of Lady Elaine, damned
to only see the world beyond
her castle windows when it was
reflected in her mirrors. If she
dared go out to see the scenery
directly, she knew she would
die. Glimpsing Sir Lancelot's
reflection during his journey
to Camelot, she fell hopelessly
in love and set out by boat to
see him. She died and Lancelot
found her body in her drifting
boat, mourning the passing of
such beauty. Thomas Mallory
located Astolat near Guildford
in *Le Morte d'Arthur* (1485).
Alfred, Lord Tennyson's 1833
lyrical ballad 'The Lady of
Shalott'(Astolat) followed suit.

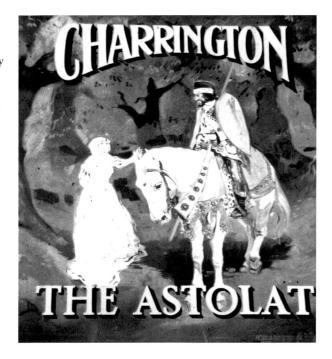

The Astronomer, Nos 125–129
Middlesex Street, E1 7JF
Prior to 2016, the pub was called
The Shooting Star. The stellar
connection comes from the building
name, Astral House, once home to
the Jewish Board of Guardians, a
charitable society for impoverished
Jewish people in London. (Courtesy
of Robby Virus)

The Bamburgh, No. 175 Bamburgh
Avenue, South Shields, NE34 6SS
In 1838, Grace Darling, daughter
of a lighthouse keeper, spotted a
ship breaking up on the rocks off
the Bamburgh coast. She and her
father took a rowing boat out at
1 a.m., rescuing nine survivors
of the *Forfarshire*. Nine other
passengers used their own lifeboat
and forty-four passengers died.

Barcadium, Nos 16–17 Fox Street, Preston, PR1 2AB
A modern bar named after the retro-arcade games played within. It has a neat beer-can sign design, though the pub name is spelt incorrectly. (Author's image)

Beltane, The Old Courthouse, George Street, Buxton, SK17 6AT
Beltane (May Day) is a Celtic pagan feast day celebrating spring, fertility and renewal. There is much dancing, drinking and seduction. In the sign a Green Man (god of the forest) can be seen observing a flirting couple through the trees to the right. (Author's image)

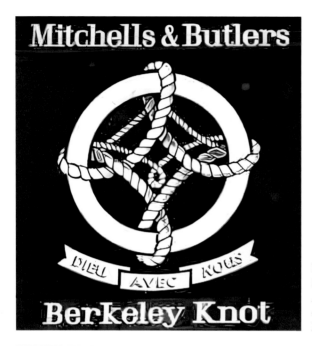

Berkeley Knot, Evesham Road, Spetchley, Worcester, WR7 4QS
A popular knot for anglers to use on their rod lines. (Courtesy of Mike Hubbard)

Betsey Trotwood, No. 56 Farringdon Road, London, EC1R 3BL
Great-aunt to Charles Dickens's eponymous hero from *David Copperfield*, Betsey begins the 1850 novel disliking men after an abusive marriage, but gradually comes to respect and aid David as his story unfolds.

**The Bishop and Wolf, Hugh Street,
St Mary's, Scilly Isles, TR21 0LL**
A double-sider. Not a cleric combatting
werewolves but a fusion of the names of
two neighbouring lighthouses, Bishop
Rock and Wolf Rock.

Bishop Blaise, No. 277 Oldham Road, Rochdale, OL16 5RD
An Armenian bishop who miraculously healed the sick and talked with animals. He was decapitated by order of Roman Emperor Licinius in 316, becoming a patron saint to veterinarians and the ill.

Black Friar, No. 174 Queen Victoria Street, Greater London, EC4V 4EG
Named after a Dominican friary, this pub and its statue sign (designed by architect Herbert Fuller-Clark) was saved from closure through a campaign led by poet John Betjeman. (Author's image)

The Blind Beggar of Bethnal Green, No. 337 Whitechapel Road, London, E1 1BU
The sign for this notorious pub (the location of the murder of one of the Kray twins) relates to the legend of Henry III supporter Henry de Montford, killed at the Battle of Evesham in 1265. In the seventeenth century a ballad surfaced claiming that Montford survived the conflict, though blinded and reduced to begging on the streets of Bethnal, guided by his dutiful daughter. (Author's image)

Blue Boar, No. 96 Deansgate, Bolton, BL1 1BD
A name rooted in the heraldic achievement of the Earl of Oxford, a supporter of the House of Lancaster, opposing Richard III – 'the White Boar'. This sign depicts a pig accidentally soaked in blue emulsion.

Blue Lias, Stockton Road, Stockton, Southam, CV47 8LD
Named after a quarry close to the pub where many dinosaur fossils have been found. Possibly the only pub sign to feature prehistoric animals.

Blue Vinny, No. 12 The Moor, Puddletown, Dorset, DT2 8TE
Dorset Blue Vinny was a popular cheese sold extensively in London until the Second World War resulted in a shortage. Black-market imitation cheeses appeared, rendering it impossible to tell genuine Blue Vinny from fakes, until the original recipe was rediscovered at a Dorset farm in the 1980s. The sign shows a punter enjoying the cheese with a pint.

Boy & Barrel, No. 8 Beast Market, Huddersfield, HD1 1QF
This 9-foot-tall sculpture sign represents a brewery dray apprentice sitting astride a beer barrel. He has been compared to Bacchus, Roman god of inebriation. (Author's image)

Brigadier Gerard, No. 84 Monkgate, York, YO31 7PF
Sherlock Holmes creator Sir Arthur Conan Doyle wrote several satirical tales of vainglorious French Hussar Brigadier Gerard, who served Napoleon in his European campaigns. The name was bestowed on a famous racehorse who won seventeen professional flat races between 1970 and 1972. (Author's image)

Bucket of Blood, No. 14 Churchtown Road, Phillack Hayle, TR27 5AE
Apocryphally inspired by the horrific discovery of a murder victim dumped down a well whose blood filled the bucket of someone innocently drawing water.

Cannard's Grave, A37, Cannard's Grave Road, Shepton Mallet, BA4 4LY
Tom Kennard (the spelling Cannard was adopted by the pub in the 1990s), a local publican, was the last man in Britain to be hanged for stealing sheep.

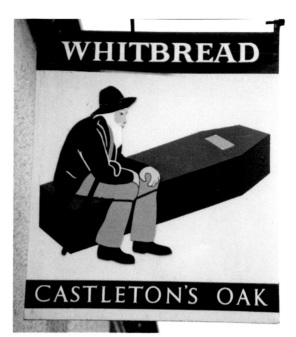

Castleton's Oak, Biddenden, Ashford, TN27 8DL
An oak tree fell near the pub on Ebeneezer Castleton's seventieth birthday. Taking it as an omen of his own impending demise, he used wood from the stricken tree to make a coffin, keeping it in his house until soon after his 100th birthday thirty years later, when he was finally interred in it.

Catherine Wheel, No. 35 Cheap Street, Newbury, RG14 5DB
The fireworks known as Catherine wheels were named after the inhumane torture and martyrdom of St Catherine on a rotating, burning wheel.

Cheshire Cheese, Nos 37–39 High Street, Buxton, SK17 6HA
These anthropomorphic mice are enjoying a wine and cheese party, complete with music. (Author's image)

Childe of Hale, No. 6 Church End, Hale, Liverpool, L24 4AX
John Middleton (1578–1623) was a true giant, with estimates declaring him 9 foot 3 inches. He had to sleep with his feet dangling out of his bedroom windows and was hired to entertain guests at the courts of the early Stuart monarchs.

The Chindit, No. 113 Merridale Road, Wolverhampton, WV3 9SE Commemorating the heroic Chindit Regiment who fought in Burma in the Second World War. The Chindits were a special operations division that were assigned missions behind Japanese lines.

The Circus Tavern, No. 86 Portland Street, Manchester, M1 4GX A travelling circus visited Manchester annually between 1795 and 1797. En route to perform in Dublin, their ship sank, leaving no survivors. The sign gives no clue as to the sad story behind the big-top spectacle depicted. (Author's image)

Coach & Horses, No. 16 West Park, Harrogate, HG1 1BJ
This 3D figure relates to the 2014 Tour de France, when a major stage of the race took place in Harrogate. This was the closest pub to the finishing line. (Author's image)

The Cockpit, No. 7 St Andrew's Hill, London, EC4V 5BY
Until its ban in 1835, pubs were popular venues for such cockfights. The Cockpit sign recreates the brutal reality of such a showdown.

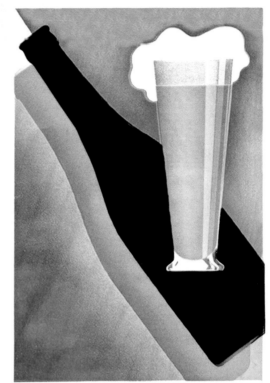

The Continental, No. 5 Meadow Lane, Preston, PR1 8JP
The optical illusion sign presents a tall glass of Continental ale with a foaming head resting on what could be a boat paddle doubling up as a bottle, resting on a second bottle. The background gives the beer head the look of a cloud in a blue sky. (Author's image)

The Craven Heifer, No. 452 Blackburn Road, Astley Bridge, Bolton, BL1 8NL
In 1807, in Gargrave, Yorkshire, a 1-ton calf was born. Her greedy owner gained fame and fortune displaying her at pubs and agricultural shows throughout England. She survived only five years of changing ownership, being constantly fed and carted round, eventually being taken on a seventy-three-day journey to London, stopping at various towns en route. Many bars, including this one in Bolton, were renamed in honour of the poor creature who was treated like a freak-show curiosity all of her short, miserable life. The sign replicates an anonymous portrait of her from 1811. (Author's image)

THE CRISPIN

The Crispin, No. 56 Grove Road, Windsor, SL4 1HS
St Crispin's feast day was 25 October, the date of the Battle of Agincourt (1415). Shakespeare's *Henry V* mentions Crispin in a morale-boosting speech to the king's men on the brink of engagement. The sign depicts Henry praying to Crispin for victory. (Author's image)

DAVENPORT ARMS

Davenport Arms (Thieves Neck), No. 550 Chester Road, Woodford, Stockport, SK7 1PS
You'll see a figure near the top of this sign with a noose around his neck. It represents a thief hanged in the eighteenth century at the very location later occupied by the pub, which was built in the following century. The Woodford Davenports employed gamekeepers to patrol their estates with permission to hang suspected poachers without trial, There's an old tree near the pub that might have been used for such executions. (Author's image)

Deacon Brodie's Tavern, No. 435 Lawnmarket, Edinburgh, EH1 2N
Deacon William Brodie (1741–88) was a respected carpenter who was commissioned to make cabinets for the wealthy. He often made duplicate keys for himself, snuck into the homes of his customers after dark and robbed them, just for fun. He was eventually caught and executed. His two-faced nice and evil nature was the inspiration for Robert Louis Stevenson's 1886 novella *Strange Case of Dr Jekyll and Mr Hyde*.

Defector's Weld, No. 170 Uxbridge Road, Shepherd's Bush, London, W12 8AA
The image here presents a tape recorder, suggesting a James Bond connection. However, it isn't fictional espionage the pub relates to but a real spy, Guy Burgess, one of the notorious 'Cambridge Five' defectors serving the KGB British secrets from respectable MI5 positions. Burgess drank here while working as a BBC broadcaster. (Author's image)

Dr Syntax, No. 1 West Road, Prudhoe, Northumberland, NE42 6HP
A bay horse from Northumberland, Doctor Syntax, won thirty-six major flat races between 1816 and 1823. His name originated in a satirical cartoon strip created by Thomas Rowlandson and William Combe in 1809 featuring the hapless adventures of Doctor (of Divinity) Syntax, who travelled Britain and pried into everyone's affairs as an interfering do-gooder and usually ended up falling in village ponds or being chased off by bulls, etc.

The Doric, Rawson Road, Waterloo, Seaforth, Liverpool, L21 1BZ
A passenger liner involved in a 1935 collision with another ship near Portugal. Unlike the *Titanic* (also owned by White Star), the *Doric*'s watertight doors functioned well and the subsequent hull breach was contained, causing only slight listing. Passengers and crew were having breakfast when rescue ships arrived. There were no fatalities, though the *Doric* was scrapped soon after being towed to port.

Left and below: The Dying Gladiator, No. 48 Bigby Street, Brigg, DN20 8EF A gladiator bleeds to death after losing his final fight. A gory image inspired by an early landlord's visit to Rome. The pub's porch statue is a reproduction of one in a Roman gallery.

The Electrical Wizard, No. 11 New Market, Morpeth, NE61 1PS
William Bodie (1869–1939) was a nineteenth-century conjurer who used electricity in his act, even faking his sister's execution in a facsimile electric chair, billed as 'La Belle Electrica'.

Eli Jenkins, Bay, Nos 7–8 Bute Crescent, Cardiff, CF10 5AN
The Revd Eli Jenkins is a character in Dylan Thomas's 1954 drama *Under Milk Wood*. Jenkins, dreaming of being a great bard, recites prayers to the sunset and renames a local hill 'Llareggub' (read it backwards). The sign depicts a drinker but without clues to his divinity or poetic ambitions.

Ensign Ewart, Nos 521–523 Lawnmarket, Edinburgh, EH1 2PE
Ensign Charles Ewart of the Scots Greys (Royal North British Dragoon Division) single-handedly captured the eagle standard of the 45th French Infantry Division, bayoneting down at least three French soldiers in the process. The eagle is on display in Edinburgh's Castle Museum.

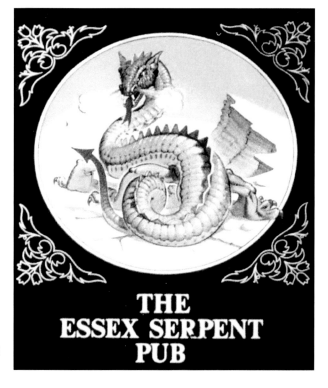

The Essex Serpent, No. 6 King Street, London, WC2E 8HN
In 1669 there were several sightings of a serpentine dragon in Saffron Walden, Essex. A 2016 novel by Sarah Perry and a 2022 TV mini-series based on this called *The Essex Serpent* draw on the serpent sightings into the Victorian era. The sign offers a beast with glistening scales, as tall as the background mountains, breathing steam and looking utterly malevolent.

The Europa, No. 171 Walton Road, Molesey, East Molesey, KT8 0DX
A Phoenician queen kidnapped and repeatedly raped by Zeus, who disguised himself as a bull to get close to her. Europa gave her name to an entire continent. Here, she is obliged to hold on tight as Zeus, still in bull form, takes a gallop.

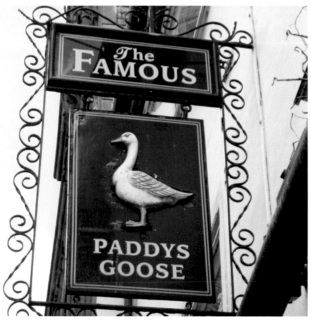

The Famous Paddy's Goose, No. 29 Bloom Street, Manchester, M1 3JE
Paddy's goose was a joke involving a duck being served as a goose to diners unable to see or taste the difference. The pub's fame lies in its ownership by brewer J. P. Joule (1818–89), who was also the scientist after whom the SI unit of energy, the Joule, was named. (Author's image)

Fanny on the Hill, Wickham Street, Welling, DA16 3DA
Fanny was a landlady of the White Horse who supposedly used pre-arranged lighting signals to warn highwayman Dick Turpin of approaching stagecoaches he might want to rob. The inn took on her name long after her death.

Finn McCóul's, No. 41 Church Road, Eccles, Manchester, M30 0BJ
McCóul accidentally gained superpowers when serving as an apprentice to the bard Finnegas, who sought the Salmon of Wisdom, believing that eating it would give him all knowledge. Catching the fish, Finnegas ordered McCóul to cook it for him, but McCóul burnt his thumb on the fish, sucking it to soothe the pain and absorbing all the wisdom himself before going on to numerous adventures. The sign pays no special attention to his thumbs.

First & Last, Wallbridge, Frome, BA11 5JX
The 'Tortoise and the Hare Race' from *Aesop's Fables* inspired this sign, showing the hare starting his run in serious athletic mode but doomed to come last after foolishly taking a nap near the finish line.

First In Last Out, Nos 14–15 High Street, Hastings, TN34 3EY
Seasoned drinkers like to be first in the pub as it opens, and last out at closing time, like a kicked-out cat sent off on a nocturnal prowl and arriving home as the milk gets delivered.

Five Alls, No. 232 Bath Road, Cheltenham, GL53 7ND
Clever wordplay, featuring a king ruling for all, a clergyman praying for all, etc., down to the working-class labourer working for all. The name was originally Four Alls – the worker was a later addition.

Flying Dutchman, No. 89 Burnley Road, Padiham, Burnley, BB12 8BL
A mariner dammed to sail the seas forever for blaspheming God. Sailors seeing his spectral ship were doomed to die in shipwrecks. The story first appeared in a 1790 book of fanciful travel tales by John Macdonald, before being used in Wagner's 1843 opera and the *Pirates of the Caribbean* movie franchise among numerous other depictions. (Author's image)

Flying Monk, No. 6 Market Place, Chippenham, SN15 3HD
Eilmer of Malmesbury was an eleventh-century base-jumping birdman, a Benedictine monk who tried to copy Icarus. He leapt from a tower with home-made wings and naturally plummeted to the ground, barely surviving and leaving both his legs shattered. Given that he lived, it indicates his wings acted as a parachute and at least decelerated his fall. The sign depicts a much more successful flight in something akin to the modern glider wingsuits used by present-day thrill-seekers, helping show that Eilmer was not as daft or suicidal as might have been supposed for generations.

Fox & Goose, Bristol Road, Brent Knoll, Highbridge, TA9 4HH
The geese (plural, despite the pub's name) hang the fox for his crimes against poultry-kind. Rather unsettling.

The Friendship Inn, Nos 278–280 Manchester Street, Werneth, Oldham, OL9 6HB
A traveller alone in Africa with only a dog for company. A milestone shows his distance from Oldham. Nearby, a puzzled lion looks on, posing no immediate threat to man or dog. (This represents Lion Ale, then the premier beer of pub owners Matthew Brown's brewery.) The weary adventurer would love a beer with his friends, but he's a solitary, vulnerable man and many leagues from home.

A newer sign for the same pub depicts an older man sitting at home with a different dog in his arms and a photo reminder that Oldham is 31 miles away (it's only 1 mile from the pub). Could this be the same traveller, safely home, fondly recalling his adventures and thinking of his old friends and pets? Possibly the only inn sign to have a sequel in a later sign for the same pub. (Both images: author's image)

The Frozen Mop, Faulkner's Lane, Mobberley, Knutsford, WA16 7AL
Inspired when a cleaner in the pub found the winter chill had frozen her mop-bucket water solid, trapping her mop there. She had to thaw it out in order to be able to do her job.

The Furze Wren, Broadway Square, No. 6
Market Place, Bexleyheath, DA6 7DY
Named after a species of Furze-bush-dwelling
bird discovered by Dr John Latham in 1773
near the site of this modern Wetherspoon's.
(Courtesy of Alison Harvey)

The Garrick Arms, Nos 8–10 Charing Cross
Road, WC2H 0HG
Burlesque dancer performing at the famous
Garrick Theatre next door, which has become
largely noted for risqué, daring productions
since staging *No Sex Please, We're British* for
four years in the 1960s. (Author's image)

Gitana's, No. 558
Hartshill Road, Hartshill,
Stoke-on-Trent, ST4 6AS
A beautiful portrait of music
hall superstar Mary Astbury,
better known by her stage
name Gertie Gitana, the
Staffordshire Cinderella. Her
signature tune was 'Nellie
Dean'.

The Goat Major, No. 33
High Street, Cardiff,
CF10 1PU
The pub has enjoyed a
long association with the
Royal Welsh Regiment,
which has a goat as its
mascot. The sign shows an
army major in full regalia,
proudly guarding the
goat, itself bedecked in the
regiment's colours.

The Grapes, No. 33 Bank Street, Melksham, SN12 6LE
A pub using a very different image than its names suggests.

Greyfriars Bobby, Nos 30–34 Candlemaker Row, Edinburgh, EH1 2QE
Named after a dog who stayed by his master's grave for fourteen years until his own death in 1872. The story was turned into a Disney movie in 1961.

Greylake Inn, Greylake, Bridgwater, Somerset, TA7 9BP
Given the inn's proximity to Glastonbury, a sign inspired by the Lady of the Lake holding Excalibur aloft isn't surprising. Hope she doesn't catch a cold.

The Gribble Inn, Gribble Lane, Oving, Chichester, PO20 2BP
The lane and brewpub are named after Oving village school teacher Rose Gribble.

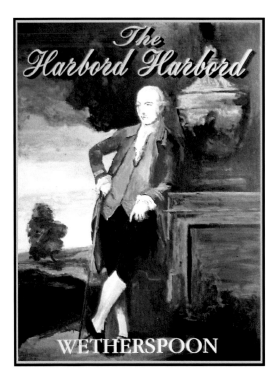

The Harbord Harbord, Nos 17–21 Long Street, Middleton, Manchester, M24 6TE
Baron Harbord Harbord (1734–1810) was related by marriage to the prominent Assheton family who ran Middleton, leading to his heavy investment in the growing township.

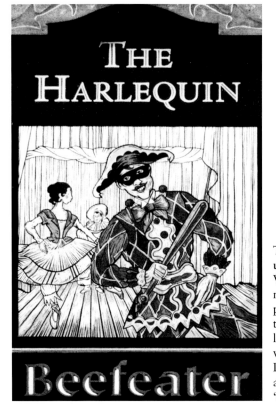

The Harlequin, Bridgefoot, Stratford-upon-Avon, CV37 7BD
When pantomime used a great deal of mime, the crowd-pleasing colourful patchwork-clothing-clad mischievous trickster Harlequin struggled to get to his lover Columbine due to various conflicts with Clown, Punch and her father, Pantaloon. He usually won, though, armed with his club, also known as the 'slapstick'.

Hawes Inn, No. 7 Newhalls Road, South Queensferry, EH30 9TA
A man drinks, oblivious that he's about to be pressed into naval service. He is David Balfour, hero of Robert Louis Stevenson's 1886 novel *Kidnapped*. Stevenson wrote the book at the Hawes Inn.

Hearts of Oak, No. 70 Boutport Street, Barnstaple, EX31 1HG
Hearts of oak are dry, solid wood at the core of oak trees – highly prized by pre-ironclad-era shipbuilders. The wood held out well under cannon-fire. Many of the ships in Nelson's fleet were made from oak heart wood. The expression 'hearts of oak' was also used to praise the bravery of the men who sailed into the heart of battle, and such a man is depicted in this sign.

Hope & Anchor, Sandy Lane, Royton, Oldham, OL2 5QP
A floating ship anchor that doesn't sink or grip the seabed is pretty useless as the ship will be at the mercy of tides, winds, storms, currents, etc. However, it symbolises Jesus, walking on water, a miraculously fixed anchor for Christian hope and faith. (Author's image)

The Hospital Inn, No. 331 Brindle Road, Bamber Bridge, Walton Summit Centre, Preston, PR5 6YP
Named after support offered on the pub's site to soldiers wounded in the Crimean War in the nineteenth century. (Author's image)

House Without a Name, Nos 75–77 Lea Gate, Bolton, BL2 3ET
The pub's first licensee arrived at the magistrates' court unsure what to call his bar. The impatient magistrate decided on the spot that its anonymity would be the name, which it remains to this day.

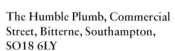

The Humble Plumb, Commercial Street, Bitterne, Southampton, SO18 6LY
Unsure what to name their new pub, its owners asked a plumber working on the bathroom facilities for suggestions. The man replied, 'Don't ask me. I'm just a humble plumb.' He returned to his duties, oblivious that he had just christened the pub. Its sign shows a plumber getting soaked by burst water pipes.

Izaak Walton, High Street, East Meon, Petersfield, GU32 1QA
Anyone into fishing may have heard of Walton as he was the author of *The Compleat Angler* (1643), which is still regarded as a classic 'how to' guide and celebration of the pastime, penned in prose and verse.

Jack Cade, Cade Street, Heathfield, TN21 9BS
Cade, of Heathfield, led an uprising against Henry IV over the high taxes imposed to fund the ongoing Hundred Years War despite hardship felt by many of the people. Cade hoped for a peaceful protest, but many marchers started looting, leading Londoners to unite with the authorities and fight against the rebels, resulting in bloodshed on London Bridge. Henry put a bounty on Cade, who was wounded while being violently arrested in Lewes, dying from his injuries while under escort to trial.

Jenny Ha's, No. 1 Browns Close, No. 65 Canongate, Edinburgh, Midlothian, EH8 8BT
Women were once forbidden from running pubs due to the belief that their presence would turn inns into brothels, but this law was overturned in 1699. Jannet Hall (Jenny Ha) was among the first women to secure a licence to run a bar in Edinburgh when the law finally came to its senses.

Jenny Lind, No. 69 High Street, Hastings, TN34 3EW
Jenny Lind was a renowned Swedish opera singer who was managed for many years by circus impresario P. T. Barnum. The pub opened in 1851 at the height of her popularity.

Jorrocks, No. 41 Iron Gate, Derby, DE1 3GA
John Horrocks was the hunt-obsessed protagonist of the *Jorrocks's Jaunts and Jollities* satires by Robert Smith Surtees, penned between 1831 and 1834. (Author's image)

Joseph Arch, No. 7 Bridge Street, Barford, Warwick, CV35 8EH
Arch founded the National Agricultural Labourers Union in 1872 and served West Norfolk as a Liberal MP from 1892 to 1900.

**Kings Stores, No. 14 Widegate,
St Bishopsgate, London, E1 7HP**
The king seems to be inviting us to share
in booze from his own special stash of
hidden barrels. The inn was actually a
military gunpowder ammunition store in the
eighteenth century. (Author's image)

**Knockerdown Inn, Knockerdown,
Ashbourne, DE6 1NQ**
Despite its formidable, seemingly invincible
warrior, the pub's name actually relates to
coal miners assigned to knocking down
overhead lumps of lime and lead to make
a new ceiling smoother while digging out
the shafts.

The Lady Luck, No. 18 St Peter's Street, Canterbury, CT1 2BQ
A glass-print femme fatale with a skull to her side, surrounded by playing cards. Luck can flip us from wealth and beauty to misfortune and death in an instant. (Author's image)

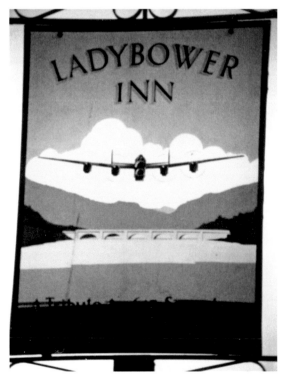

Ladybower, A57, Hope Valley, S33 0AX
A Lancaster bomber flies over the Ladybower Reservoir, commemorating the 70th anniversary of its use as a testing site for the 'Bouncing Bomb' Dam Buster air raid of 1943.

The Lambton Worm, North Road, Chester-le-Street, DH3 4AJ
Inspired by the ballad *The Lambton Worm*. It tells of young John Lambton skiving off church one Sunday to go fishing, despite a witch's warnings that this would bring forth great sorrow. Lambton caught a strange worm and kept it as a pet until it grew too big, then cast it into a village well. It thrived, growing into a terrible monster and terrorising Durham. Lambton returned from the Crusades with much more courage than when he left and killed the creature in true St George tradition.

Lamorna Wink, Lamorna Cove, Lamorna, Penzance, TR19 6XQ
Source of the smuggling nod 'tipping the wink', a coded body language signal that contraband goods can be collected.

The Land 'O' Cakes, No. 58 Lever Street, Manchester, M1 1FJ
A name meaning 'Scotland', drawn from Robert Burns's 1789 poem 'On the Late Captain Grose's Peregrinations Thro' Scotland'.

> Hear, Land o'Cakes, and brither Scots,
> Frae Maidenkirk ro Johnnie Groat's;-

The Lanivet, Truro Road, Lanivet, Bodmin, PL30 5ET
Signs for this pub have always depicted giant pandas, and the local football team are known as 'The Pandas'. The reason is because bamboo is grown in the area to feed the pandas at London Zoo.

The Lass of Richmond Hill, No. 8 Queen's Road, Richmond, TW10 6JJ
The lass in the Richmond Hill ballad song heralds from Richmond in Yorkshire. The phrase 'A rose without a thorn' comes from the song. The lyric was penned by Leonard McNally. His 'lass' was Frances I'Anson, who died in childbirth five years into their marriage.

Latymers, No. 157 Hammersmith Road, London, W6 8BS
The sign confuses William Latymer, friend and biographer of Anne Boleyn, and the later Hugh Latimer, one of three Oxford Martyrs – Anglican bishops burnt at the stake on the orders of Mary, Queen of Scots in 1555. William Latymer died much more peacefully.

The Letter B, Church Street, Whittlesey, Peterborough, PE7 1DE
Young sweethearts and no letters in sight. The last of a trio of pubs. Companion bars Letters A and C closed down.

Liz 'n' Lil's, No. 78 King William Street, Ewood, Blackburn, BB1 7EB
Blackburn's Liz and Lil are dancing around, possibly not entirely sober, during a happy night out. (Author's image)

Merry Widows, No. 24 Railway Terrace, Derby, DE1 2RU
The Derby Widows, possibly by the same artist as the sign above, look younger and happy despite the loss of their husbands. (Author's image)

Load of Mischief, South Street, Blewbury, Didcot, Oxfordshire, OX11 9PX
Attributed to eighteenth-century artist William Hogarth, this sign controversially depicts a man carrying his gin-drinking wife on his shoulders. A monkey tweaks his ear as a representation of endless nagging. The padlocked chain round his neck says 'wedlock'.

Lollards Pit, Nos 69–71 Riverside Road, Norfolk, NR1 1SR
A pub built directly on top of the site of the infamous 1531 religious massacres, when local Lollards (pre-Protestant critics of Catholicism) were denounced as heretics, taken to a chalk pit and burnt to death at the stake. A plaque on the pub wall commemorates the atrocity.

**The Lord Moon of the Mall,
Nos 16–18 Whitehall, London**
There is no Lord Moon. The
portrait subject is Tim Martin, the
controversial pro-Brexit founder
of J. D. Wetherspoon. Perhaps he
hopes to be granted a peerage for his
services. (Author's image)

**Maggie Murphy's, Bath Street,
Glasgow, G2 4UZ**
Depicted as a young harpist, Maggie
was believed to be a hideous old
hag who ran a home for unruly
children, subjecting them to corporal
punishments. She never existed. She
was a bogeyman-type figure that
Scottish parents frightened their
children with: 'Behave or you're going
to Maggie's.'

The Major from Glengarry,
Nos 10–14 Upper Church Road,
Weston-super-Mare, BS23 2DT
Major Alastair MacDonell was a
Jacobite, arrested trying to join the
1745 Rebellion, serving two years
in the Tower of London before
infiltrating the Jacobites as a spy
acting in the interests of the British
authorities. The motto translates to
'By sea, by land'.

Margaret Catchpole, Cliff Lane,
Ipswich, IP3 0PQ
Margaret Catchpole (1762–1819)
was a Sussex born and bred servant
girl. Plunged into poverty, she stole
a horse and rode to London hoping
to unite with her sweetheart, but
she was arrested and deported to
Australia, where her chronicles
became an important record of
Australian social history.

Marie Lloyd, No. 289 Mare Street, Hackney, London, E8 1EJ
Marie Lloyd was renowned for her often risqué music hall songs, notably 'Oh Mr Porter What Shall I Do?' and her best-known number, 'My Old Man Said Follow the Van'. She died of kidney failure in 1922, aged fifty-two.

Martha Gunn, No. 100 Upper Lewes Road, Brighton, BN2 3FE
When Georgian sea swimmers required bathing machines to discreetly change clothes for water-wear, dippers like Martha Gunn assisted them in getting in and out of the water.

Minerva, Nelson Street, Hull, HU1 1XE
The name comes from Roman mythology; Minerva is the goddess of wisdom. She is often portrayed conversing with owls, hence many depictions of 'wise owls' in art, literature and films, and on several pub signs.

Molly Mogg's, No. 2 Old Compton Street, London, W1D 4TA
Molly was a barmaid at The Rose pub in Wokingham, Sussex, who inspired poet John Gay to write a ballad in 1726 about a customer who was infatuated with her. Fellow bards Alexander Pope and Dean Swift added lines too.

Moon & Sixpence, No. 1 Bernard Street, Glossop, Derbyshire, SK13 7AA
Originally called The Fleece when it opened in 1846, it was renamed after a 1919 novel by W. Somerset Maugham. The book is loosely based on the life of the Impressionist artist Paul Gauguin, with its title referring to how if you look on the ground hoping to find misplaced fallen sixpences, you miss the glory of the rich moonlight above. (Author's image)

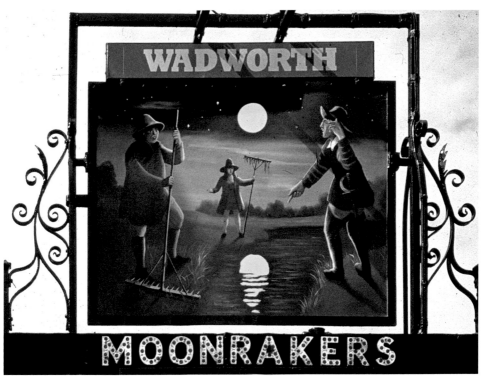

Moonrakers, No. 57 High Street, Pewsey, SN9 5AF
Urban legend tells of drunks from the pub seeing the reflection of the moon in a nearby river and assuming it was drowning. They tried to fish it out of the water with garden rakes.

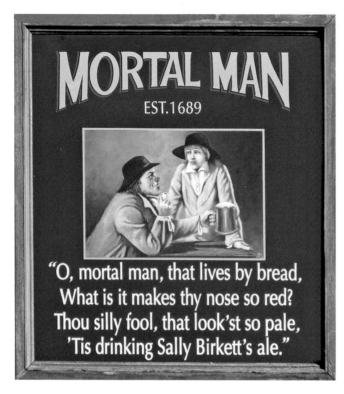

Mortal Man, Troutbeck, Windermere, LA23 1PL
Called The White House when it first opened in 1689, it was renamed *c*. 1900 due to the local popularity of the Sally Birkett ballad quoted on the sign. The men depicted were customers in the pub who posed for the artist.

The Moses Gate, No. 5 Bolton Road, Farnworth, BL4 7JU
This has nothing to do with the biblical patriarch, but means 'The way through the moss'. The pub is close to Moses Gate Country Park, near Bolton, which has many woodland and wetland features.

The Muddled Man, Lower Street, West Chinnock, TA18 7PT

A tenant struggling to think of a new pub name wrote out a list to discuss with his wife, who was recuperating in hospital at the time. Entering the ward, he dropped his notes. As he recovered them he apologised to the staff for being such a 'muddled man', to which one nurse suggested that ought to be the name of the pub, and so it is.

The Murderers, Nos 2–8 Timber Hill, Norwich, NR1 3LB

There was only one murderer, Frank Miles, who killed his ex-wife in a fit of jealousy in 1895 after she flirted with another man in the pub where she worked. He notified the police of the crime himself, escaping the gallows but dying in prison ten years later.

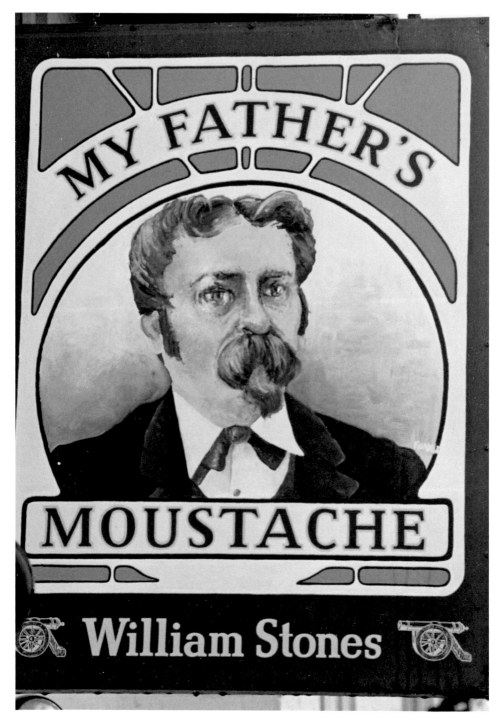

My Father's Moustache, North Holme Road, Louth, LN11 0HF
A unique pub name with a simple origin. The publican, seeking a new name for the bar, asked his children for suggestions. Pointing to his impressive moustache, the children coined the name that has adorned the establishment ever since.

Nags Head, No. 41 Church Street,
Eccles, Salford, M30 0BJ
A double-sided sign with an old horse
on one half and controversy on the
other in the form of an angry-looking
lady with a rolling pin, indicative of
a nagging wife from the kind of jokes
that would now be regarded as sexist
and politically incorrect. (Both images:
author's image)

New Britannia Inn, No. 6 Heatley Street, Preston, PR1 2XB

The pub is named after the Roman word for Britain. Britannia eventually became personified as a Roman goddess, symbolising the conquest of Britain. Interest in her was revived in 1665, thanks to diarist Samuel Pepys. He got a model to pose in Britannia's armour for a new farthing coin, in what is now the archetypal image of the goddess. The model was Frances Stewart, a concubine of Charles II. The image is copied, often with little variation, on many British inn signs. A later sign for the pub does provide some variation by removing the ocean water featured in the earlier version. Maybe the tide went out. A yet newer sign adds a magnificent stone lion as a companion to the goddess. (All images: author's image)

Nine Giants, Thornhill Road, Cardiff, CF14 6PE
Not the solitary giant, but the massive trees he is tending. The area was noted for the trees surrounding the property, originally named The Lissadrone. Some of the trees are still there.

Nine Saxons, Oakridge Centre, Basingstoke, RG21 5LG
In 1965–66, archaeologists at a dig in Basingstoke unearthed nine Romano-British human skulls in an abandoned well. The skulls were wrongly referred to as Saxon in origin by the local media and gave their name to this now closed local estate pub, which later developed some reputation for violent altercations. Many locals called it 'The Nine Stab Wounds'.

Nowhere, No. 21 Gilwell Street, Plymouth, PL4 8BU
A great name for a pub where the drinker, unwilling to disclose his location to someone asking where he is going (or went to), can easily snap back 'Nowhere', thus telling the truth and also saying 'none of your business'. The sign shows direction markers pointing to Nowhere whichever way you travel, making the pub the only place to be.

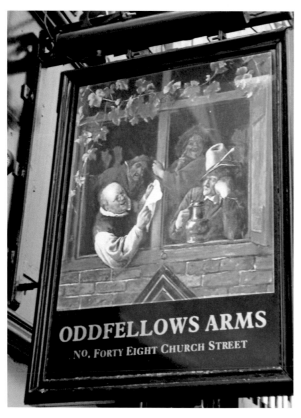

Oddfellows Arms, Church Street, Eccles, Salford, M30 0BJ
I frequently say pub signs are works of art, and this one more than qualifies in recreating Dutch Master Jan Steen's *Rhetoricians at a Window* (*c.* 1664), a study of eccentric larger-than-life Bohemian actors presenting a live show through the window of an inn. The Oddfellows Society is a quasi-Masonic benevolent organisation that uses pubs for its meetings and social events. (Author's image)

The Old Bill and Bull, No. 1312 Coventry Road, Birmingham, B25 8AW
A photo-realistic sign reflecting a simple history. The Bull pub became a police station, and 'Old Bill' is common slang for policemen. The building was then turned back into a pub. The alliteration of Bill and Bull lent itself easily to the bar's name. (Author's image)

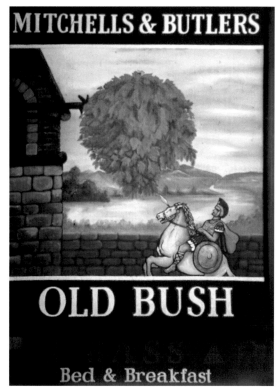

The Old Bush, Walsall Road, Pelsall, Walsall, WS3
The Romans introduced pub signage in the form of bushes pressed into the thatch of inns and taverns they liked. The song 'The Old Bull and Bush' derives from this practice.

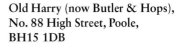

Old Harry (now Butler & Hops), No. 88 High Street, Poole, BH15 1DB
Harry Paye was a fifteenth-century pirate, plundering loot from French and Spanish ships, often just for devilment. In retaliation for his attacks on their coastal towns, the French and Spanish navies united for a 1405 raid on his native Poole. They were successfully driven off by the locals. Harry rewarded the townsfolk for their spirited defence by taking 12,000 gallons of French wine for them from a galleon he raided on his very next expedition.

Old House at Home, Albion Street, Cleckheaton BD19 3DJ
A name taken from a nostalgic sentimental ballad penned by Thomas Haynes Bayley and set to music in 1838. The song became popular with soldiers fighting far from home and longing to get back safely. (Author's image)

The Old Tower, No. 6 Sandford Street, Radcliffe, M26 2PT The sign depicts the building work on Radcliffe Castle's keep tower before it opened in 1403, during the reign of Henry IV, as a manorial home for Lord James de Radcliffe. (Author's image)

Paul Pry, No. 1023 Lincoln Road, Walton, Peterborough, PE4 6AH A name inspired by the popular stage farce *Paul Pry* (1825) by John Poole about the exploits of a nosey parker.

Peggy Gadfly's, No. 93 Victoria Street, New Brighton, CH45 2JB
Exploiting the loss of a leg, Peggy would invite passers-by to throw coins off the New Brighton Pier. He would then dive into the sea to salvage the money which he kept as a reward for his stunt, one he repeated several times a day for the growing crowds he attracted.

Percy Hobbs, Alresford Road, Winchester, Hampshire, SO21 1HL
A man with no claim to historic importance beyond drinking for sixty-three years in a bar (formerly The New Inn) that put his portrait and name on its sign.

Peveril of the Peak, No. 127 Great Bridgewater Street, Manchester, M1 5JQ
An unusual inn name, drawn from a record-breaking Manchester to London stagecoach that ran from the pub. The stagecoach itself got the name from an eponymous Walter Scott novel. The sign portrait may be an illustration from the book. (Author's image)

Phantom Coach, Fletchamstead Highway, Canley, Coventry, CV4 7BA
This pub is associated with an apocryphal stagecoach that crashed off the road into a swamp, drowning everyone on board. It's still seen, and sometimes just heard, re-running its final tragic ride by the pub, which is supposedly built on land reclaimed from the mire.

Picketty Witch, No. 147 Ilchester Road, Yeovil, Somerset, BA21 3BG
The name has nothing to do with witchcraft, despite the sign. It relates to a wych elm tree situated on a triangular corner of land known in Old English as a *piccede*. The 1960s pop group Pickettywitch took their name from the pub, in which they drank.

The Pump & Truncheon, No. 170 Station Road, Bamber Bridge, Preston, PR5 6TP
The Bamber Bridge pub was once a police station. Its sign depicts a jolly policeman for who 'not drinking on duty' means nothing. He holds one foaming beer while pouring another from the pump, with his truncheon in its holster and his helmet on his head. (Author's image)

Pearsons, No. 72 Market Street, Chorley, PR7 2SE
The Pearsons sign in Chorley comes from the same artist and depicts the same scene minus the police uniform. Such recycling is not unknown with sign creators. (Author's image)

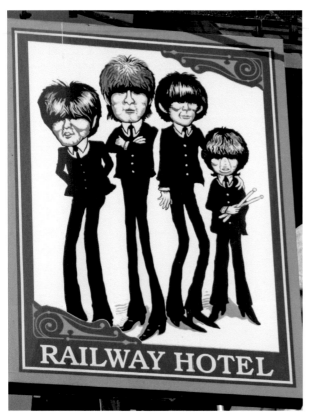

Railway Hotel, Pillory Street, Nantwich, CW5 5SS
Most railway pub signs feature trains. This one instead offers an unmistakable portrait of The Beatles, simply marking the pub's status as a popular live-music venue. (Courtesy of Chris Brooks)

Ram Jam, A1 Northbound, Stretton, Oakham, LE15 7QX
Supposedly named after an early ruse played by a young Dick Turpin before his status as a major highwayman was established. Seeing a barmaid was struggling to change a barrel, he offered to help, advising her to press her fingers into the barrel tap's spigot holes, which caused her to get her fingers jammed, at which point Turpin fled the pub without settling his drinks tab. She was unable to chase after him or report the crime until someone turned up to free her. It is precisely this ingenious stunt that is depicted on the sign.

The 1960s UK pop band Ram Jam (not to be confused with a 1970s US band of the same name) is believed to take its name from the pub. The author Margaret Drabble has been a frequent visitor. (Courtesy of Chris Brooks)

Rattlebone, Church Street, Sherston, North Wiltshire, SN16 0LR
A formidable early eleventh-century warrior serving with the forces of Edmund Ironside in his ultimately doomed campaigns against King Cnut. John Rattlebone had his stomach slashed open, but supposedly pressed a stone slab over the wound with one hand to keep his guts in while he slaughtered several more of Cnut's men, forcing the king into a (temporary) retreat.

The Rock, Hoath Corner, Chiddingstone Hoath, Edenbridge, TN8 7BS
The area is named after a large natural rock formation known as the Chiding Stone, believed to have been used as a place where women accused of gossip would be taken, sat down and chided (insulted and stared at) by the villagers. The naked lady in the sign is rather happier and more relaxed as she enjoys the summer freedom of the countryside.

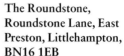

The Roundstone, Roundstone Lane, East Preston, Littlehampton, BN16 1EB
During the Industrial Revolution a watermill's wheel rolled downhill and killed a chap who just happened to get in its path. Though his body was taken away for burial, the wheel was left where it fell until it was removed in the early twentieth century. Prior to the start of the Second World War in 1939, the inn opened where the wheel had been and took a name linked to the tragedy, as does the lane the pub is situated on.

Running Pump, Catforth Road, Preston, PR4 0HH
The pub was built on a marsh and required constant pumping to drain the water seeping up into the cellars, so the pump was in operation 24/7, giving its name to the inn. Sadly, it did not survive the Covid-19 lockdown period during 2020.

St Margarets Tavern, No. 389 Bury Old Road, Prestwich, Manchester, M25 1QA
The name comes from the nearby Victorian St Margaret's Church, which was almost called St Thomas's, but as that name was suggested by the 2nd Earl of Wilton, who just happened to have the name Thomas Egerton, St Margaret was chosen instead, much to the vain Earl's chagrin.

The Sally Pussey, Swindon Road, Royal Wootton Bassett, Swindon, SN4 8ET
A formidable, humourless landlady at the pub previously known as The Wheatsheaf, Sarah Purse (her sign name derives from it) would punch out unruly male customers. She also believed in faith-healing, which she practised on people, pets and livestock in the community. She ran the pub until her death in 1885. The sign looks posed, as if she is impatient to get back on duty behind the bar as the artist finishes his work, though the new name and sign did not appear until the 1970s.

Samson & Lion, No. 140 Brierley Hill Road, Stourbridge, Brierley Hill, DY8 5SP
Samson's superhero-like strength is well known from the Old Testament's Book of Judges, where he allegedly killed a lion with his bare hands. What makes his appearance on a pub sign surprising is that Samson was a member of an obscure Jewish religious order called the Nazarites. Members were strictly teetotal, so he would have wanted nothing to do with pubs.

Ship Centurion Arminus, No. 111 High Street, Whitstable, CT5 1AY
One of the most unusual pub names in the UK, and it has no connection to Roman centurions
or the Latin language. The pub opened in 1750 and was for many years called simply The Ship,
though it had an early sign depicting a ship called *The Centurion*. This was a naval vessel that
circumnavigated the globe between 1770 and 1774 under the command of Captain George
Anson. The crew were severely decimated by starvation and dysentery (the five other ships on
the expedition perished with all hands) but *The Centurion* eventually captured a gold-laden
Spanish galleon, making Anson and his crew extremely wealthy. It is believed that the pub was
first opened by a survivor from the voyage.

As for the 'Arminus' part of the name: well, the pub would later be run by husband and wife
Jan and Armin Birks.

Sixteen String Jack, Coppice Row, Theydon Bois, Epping, CM16 7DS
Highwayman John ('Jack the Lad') Rann was noted for his dandy lifestyle and habitual wearing of sixteen colourful string bands around his silk stockings. Quite the womaniser, he even entertained some of his admirers in Newgate Prison on the eve of his execution at Tyburn in 1774, aged just twenty-four.

The Skirrid, Llanvihangel Crucorney, Abergavenny, NP7 8DH
The pub, which claims to be the oldest in Wales, takes its name from the nearby Skirrid Mountain, here depicted being struck and split apart by a thunderbolt. Legend has it that the mountain was shattered on the instant of Christ's death on the cross. It is more likely that the sheared-away sectioning was caused by glacial action during the ice ages.

The Snakecatcher, Lyndhurst Road, Brockenhurst, SO42 7RL
Harry 'Brusher' Mills, born in 1840, lived most of his life in a charcoal burner's hut in the New Forest. He caught snakes – usually alive – for sale to London Zoo, medical research groups and on behalf of anyone hiring him to rid their cellars of the creatures. He is believed to have caught up to 30,000 grass snakes and adders in his remarkable life. He was a regular customer in the Railway Inn and died heading home after a night out there. The pub changed its name in tribute to him.

The Snooty Fox, Market Place, Tetbury, GL8 8DD
The White Hart, Tetbury, offered hospitality to members of the Beaufort Hunt for many years. After they criticised the landlord, Maxwell Joseph, for being working class rather than gentry, the 1970s publican barred them all, renaming the pub The Snooty Fox in memory of their snobbery.

Solomon Grundy, No. 56 Upper Street, London, N1 0NY
Inspired by a nursery rhyme character who lived his
entire life in a single week.

The Spite, No. 1 Roebuck Lane, Newall with Clifton, Otley, LS21 2EY
Though officially called The Roebuck, this bar delights in
a nickname from its earlier years. The owner of the pub
resented it when another pub, The Traveller's Inn, opened
a few hundred yards up the road. In 1953, William
Parkinson, a regular at The Traveller's, was seen drinking
in The Roebuck. He was barred from The Traveller's for
life. Parkinson was uncomfortable with the bitter friction
between the publicans of the two bars, referring to the
miserable atmosphere of 'malice and spite' that was
engendered. This led to The Traveller's Inn being called
The Malice and The Roebuck rechristened The Spite,
which stuck long after The Malice closed down. The inn
is no longer spiteful or unwelcoming.

Stand Up Inn, No. 47 High Street, Lindfield, RH16 2HN
Temperance teetotallers criticised drinkers who stood
rather than taking a seat, as they believed that you
got inebriated more quickly in a less-relaxed, vertical
posture. Several pubs once provided few seats because
standing customers spent their money more quickly.
That was not Edward Durant's motive in providing
very few stools for his clientele, however. He was also a
leading draper and brewer and allowed his staff to have
a drink in his pub on their breaks, but he wanted to be
sure that they didn't get too comfortable so they would
drink up and get back to their workstations when their
shifts recommenced. He openly advocated 'perpendicular
drinking'. The pub now provides chairs for its customers.

Starving Rascal, No. 1 Brettell Lane, Amblecote, Stourbridge, DY8 4BN
Early in the twentieth century (the pub then called the Dudley Arms) the landlord turned away a beggar pleading for shelter at the inn one winter night. He found the beggar frozen to death on the pub's doorstep the following morning. His ghost still allegedly haunts the inn.

Swan Hotel, Thornthwaite, Keswick, CA12 5SQ
This pub's conventional swan sign and name totally bypass
the best story associated with the inn. In 1783, the Bishop
of Derry got drunk in the pub and gambled that he could
ride his horse right up the nearby steep gradient Barf Fell.
A stone marks the impressively high point he reached
before both bishop and horse fell to their deaths in the
attempt. The pub avoided the temptation to change the
name it had before local history was made there.

**Thames Head, No. 12 Albert Embankment, Lambeth,
North London, SE1 7TJ**
The spade-bearing Old Father Thames deity is reminiscent
of the Greek god Poseidon's representation in the 1963 film
Jason and the Argonauts.

**Tiddy Dols, No. 55 Shepherds Market, Mayfair, London,
WL1 7PN**
Tiddy was an eighteenth-century gingerbread seller in
London, immortalised in the William Hogarth engraving
The Idle Prentice Executed at Tyburn. Tiddy can be seen in
the foreground selling his wares to the crowd gathering to
watch the executions.

The Thomas Ingoldsby, Nos 5–9
Burgate, Canterbury, CT1 2HG
Ingoldsby was a Canterbury citizen
and author of the *Ingoldsby Legends*
(1840–47), a popular series of poems
and stories about ghosts and imps
(like the one adorning the pub's sign).
(Author's image)

The Treacle Mine, Hailsham Road,
Polegate, Eastbourne, BN26 6QL
An obvious nonsense name, but legend
has it that in 1853 soldiers from the
barracks at Chobham Common in
Surrey hid several barrels of treacle
thick molasses in the camp grounds
while they went off to fight in the
Crimea. Unfortunately, the local
villagers dug them up, mining the
ground to steal the stash. Various
other towns have seized on the
idea, including this Eastbourne pub
in Polegate.

The Trusty Servant, Minstead, Lyndhurst, Hampshire, SO43 7FY
This is the weirdest sign for any pub I've seen. The servant has a pig snout, deer legs, donkey ears and a padlocked mouth, suggesting someone had little regard or respect for domestic butlers, valets, waiters, etc. The sign actually replicates a painting created by John Hoskins for the nearby Winchester College in 1579. The original painting bears a verse explaining the anachronisms. The padlock represents the servant's obligation to keep his master's secrets. The deer legs are for swiftness in going about his duties. The sword symbolises his willingness to fight for the protection of his employers and their property. The snout is a sneering reference to his private dining habits: 'The Porker's snout not nice in diet shows.'

Twa Corbies, No. 40 Kilbowie Road, Cumbernauld, Glasgow, G67 2PX
A name based on a macabre anonymous Scottish ballad in which carrion crows discuss the rotting unburied corpse of a noble knight in a nearby field. The cause of death is unknown, though his widow has abandoned him for another man without even arranging a funeral, implying that she may have been instrumental in his demise. The birds delight in the veritable banquet, with one looking forward to chewing out the knight's eyes. The sign shows the dead knight in full body armour as the birds debate their feast within sight of him from a drystone wall.

Upton Muggery, No. 58 Old Street, Upton-upon-Severn, Worcester, WR8 0HW
Upton is the name of the village, which seems obvious, while Muggery comes from the pub's unique extensive and ever-expanding collection of drinking mugs that cover the ceiling and make dusting the place quite a challenge. The sign shows a customer cheerfully holding up one of the mugs.

Vinyl Tap, No. 30 Adelphi Street, Preston, PR1 7BE
A simple record design representing the pub's dedication to playing original vinyl and live music rather than piped music and digital downloads. The name cleverly puns the 1984 film *This Is Spinal Tap*. This is a new pub and bucks the trend for taprooms and café bars having no inn signs at all in an effort to be trendy. These give the impression of being alternatives to a pub at a time when many pubs and bars are closing at a frightful rate. (Author's image)

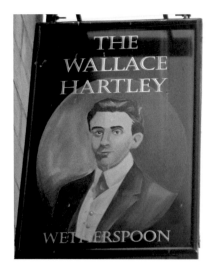

The Wallace Hartley, Nos 35–37 Church Street, Colne, BB8 0EB
The sign shows a handsome young man in suit and tie, offering no clues to his heroic, tragic fate. Born in Colne, he was the bandleader who inspired the eight-man orchestra to play on during the sinking of the *Titanic* in 1912 in a bid to keep the stricken passengers from panicking. None of the musicians survived the disaster. Hartley had proposed marriage to a girl called Maria Robinson just before sailing. A man to be truly proud of. (Author's image)

We Three Loggerheads, Ruthin Roadd, Loggerheads, Mold, CH7 5LH
Nearly everyone seeing this will say to themselves, 'I see only two people. Where's the third?' The answer is that it's you, troubling yourself contemplating the riddle.

Weavers Answer, No. 74 Milnrow Road, Shaw, Oldham, OL2 8ER
What was the question, let alone the answer? Is the reply to order the young apprentice back to his workstation or a more sympathetic, constructive, positive response? The answer is actually a riddle relating to the name of the pub itself, and refers simply to the word on the entrance mat: 'Welcome'. (Author's image)

The Wellington, No. 40 Glover's Court, Preston, PR1 3LS
The Wellington, No. 120 Regent Road, Salford, M5 3GY
Preston's sign was unique, though it has now been sadly replaced by a quite conventional portrait of the Duke of Wellington. This earlier sign actually had a real Wellington boot sliced in two and pinned up on either side of the sign board. I love the cheeky humour of the Ordsall sign. Quite a lot of signs present the Duke's portrait, often copied from official paintings of him. This sign cleverly turns him into a living Wellington boot, grinning while looking through a field telescope. (Author's images)

The Wheelbarrow Castle, Alcester Road, Radford, Worcester, WR7 4LR
Popular with Roundhead troops in the English Civil War after they secured the area in 1642. It's claimed that barrows were stored at the pub to wheel drunken officers home to their barracks at closing time.

The White Horse, No. 1 High Street, Chichester, PO18 9HX
A cat? Surely there has been some mistake. Well, not exactly. A pub proprietor knew a local artist and invited her to paint him a new White Horse sign, but she confessed that the only animals she could confidently paint were cats, so they decided it might be fun to add a cat image despite the equine name.

The White Lion, No. 135 Buxton Road, Disley, Stockport, SK12 2HA Most White, Red and Golden Lion pubs have signs showing the lion in central detail, realistically or heraldically. This enigmatic sign shows the lion as a spectral white silhouette while focussing attention on the zebras endangered by its presence. (Author's image)

The Who'd Ha Thought It, No. 9 Baker Street, Rochester, ME1 3DN 'I'll believe it when pigs fly' refers to something highly unlikely to ever take place, such as the election of an honest politician. This Rochester pub makes the magical day a reality by presenting a winged porker flying over a farm.

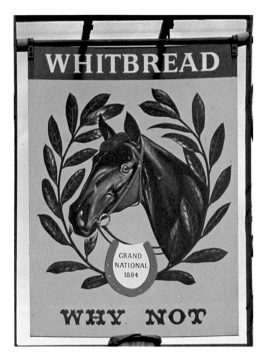

Why Not, No. 141 Broad Lane, Essington, Wolverhampton, WV11 2RH
This pub, dating from *c*. 1860, was originally called Why Not Come In and See? This was obviously a great invitation for passers-by to check out what was on offer within. The name was shortened to 'Why Not' when a racehorse of that name won the 1894 Grand National.

The Will Adams, No. 73 Saxton Street, Gillingham, ME7 5EG
Originally called The Anglo-Saxon, the pub was renamed in honour of Will Adams, an Englishman who became a fully trained Japanese samurai warrior – hence the fierce sword and armour bearer on the sign. Adams's life was the inspiration for James Clavell's epic 1975 novel *Shogun*.

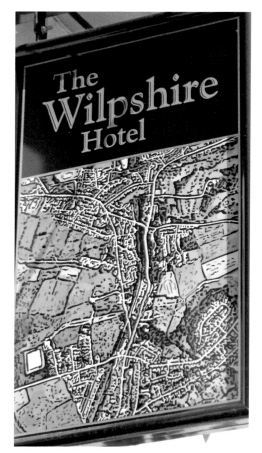

The Wilpshire Hotel, No. 7 Whalley Road, Wilpshire, Blackburn, BB1 9LQ
It became trendy in the 1980s for people to buy aerial photographs of their neighbourhood, and we are now used to seeing aircraft and drone images of towns, villages, etc., on Google Maps. The Wilpshire may be the first pub to make use of such a photo for its pub sign. Neat idea. (Author's image)

Wooden Doll, Hudson Street, North Shields, NE30 1JS
A portrayal involving a statue unusually designed to be broken apart for good luck. The original 'Wooden Doll' was a ship's figurehead that a man called Alexander Bartleman salvaged and transformed into a statue for the town in 1814. It soon became a tradition for mariners due to sail to chip bits off the 'Dolly' as good luck charms. The Dolly has had to be fully replaced five times to date. At a time when controversial statues have been trashed in acts of political protest, a statue designed for vandalising (by sailors only) is a breath of fresh air. The pub sign preserves the Dolly image more permanently.

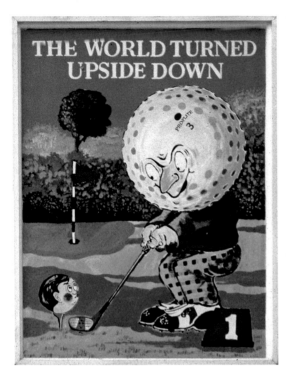

**The World Turned Upside Down,
No. 87 Basingstoke Road, Reading,
Berkshire, RG2 0JE**
A nonsensical idea where a golf ball
plays golf with a human head on the
golf tee. The ball has a malicious,
vengeful, 'see how you like it'
expression. Funny and creepy.

**Ye Olde Murenger House, No. 52
High Street, Newport, NP20 1GA**
A murenger was a collector of tolls
used to maintain town walls. Historians
dispute whether Newport ever had
walls surrounding the town or not.
Sixteenth-century poet John Leyland
said there were no town walls, while
nineteenth-century historian William
Coxe said there were. The chap here
may therefore be a product of the
artist's imagination.